Thriving in the Midst of Uncertainty

A Strategic Conversation

with Bill Watkins

The Transition Chronicles

By Dr. Ed Brenegar

The Transition Chronicles

An Imprint of Circle of Impact Press
Thriving in the Midst of Uncertainty:
A Strategic Conversation with Bill Watkins

ISBN (ebook): 978-1-7350656-4-9
ISBN (print): 978-1-7350656-9-4

Ed Brenegar

CIRCLE OF IMPACT

Circle of Impact Press
Jackson Hole, Wyoming
Published in the United States

Table of Contents

Time and again, we hear people advocating being "agents of change." I don't know what they are talking about. Their idea of change is just too vague and general for me. For too many, it is just talk without substantive action. Show me your change. What difference are you truly making? Don't give me a marketing pitch. Tell me straight. Be specific, I am going to change what in the next 90 days? Then, and only then, will I believe that you understand what change is.

What is change? The passage of time? Change of seasons? Ending of one thing and the start of another? Is it a change in our perception? Or, is it putting everything on the table and saying, "I am willing to give up all of this, right here, in order to create the change, the impact that truly makes a difference that matters?" What you are willing to invest, to sacrifice for change, is really the only credibility that we bring to our lives and work when we talk about change.

I have been studying change through the lens of leadership most of my adult life. Most of what I read about change has not been helpful. It just feels like something that they have only experienced in some safe, protective way.

What has worked for me is conversation with people. I talk with people every day about the transitions that they are going through. They've taught me not to not see change, but transition. They show the many tiny little steps of change along a pathway from one place to another that brought them to this place in their lives. Listen to people and you can discern the meaning of their change as hard, sometimes traumatic, and amazingly liberating. Almost every one of these people needs help to learn how to function in the midst of change, and more importantly, how to function in it. This is what transition is like.

We are all in transition. The transition that we are in is accelerating and becoming more critical. Our world is fragile and dangerous in ways that almost none of us have ever experienced. We are moved out of a time where linear, binary thinking, meaning one-thing-follows another in a slow, predictable manner, and good versus bad no longer explains what is taking place. There is a disorientation developing that is making it difficult to choose what to do every day. For many people the gift of shelter-in-place was that they could hide from the realities that are before us now.

The Transition Chronicles series is about the changes we are experiencing. In this short book, I want to narrow our focus on change and transition to what it means to experience uncertainty. Change and transition feels like something in time. Uncertainty feels more personal, more about who I am and how I fit in the circumstances that are going on. Feeling uncertain impacts who we see ourselves and the decisions we make about our families and our businesses.

In this contribution to the series, I have a conversation with my friend and colleague, Bill Watkins of The Lions Pride. Bill is a coach, teacher, and a leader in the field of accelerating business growth and personal growth (at the same time!). His background is as world-class cyclist, West Point graduate, decorated veteran and successful business owner. He would also say supportive husband and proud dad. He has distilled his experience in life and business down to some very insightful disciplines which make a difference that matters. He is a person of immense wisdom and practicality. He is a model of a person of impact whom I am glad to call my friend.

I invited him to talk with me about what he is seeing as he coaches business leaders and Founder CEOs. He's sharing some essentials of what I believe you will find helpful as you address the daily challenges of change.

Uncertainty, the other constant?

Our conversation began talking about how we were managing the life during the initial months of the COVID-19 coronavirus pandemic. Then we moved right into talking about why I invited him to talk with me.

Bill: ... what you want me to talk about is ...

Ed: Yes.

Bill: ... the future ... Ed, you know this, you and I both know the future is always un-certain. I don't know why during corona-

virus we just started to talk about all this uncertainty. Yes, we're amidst this period of uncertainty, but Dude, when was it ever certain? It wasn't. It never was.

We just felt like it was certain because it seemed predictable. But chaos theory tells us that when a butterfly flaps its wings in Brazil ... Boom ... Something happens in our neighborhood.

What we had to pivot into was a mindset of a future that is always uncertain. What is predictable are the resources that you have at hand to manage change and uncertainty. The A player team that you have to execute the strategic plan that you can pivot in an agile way towards ... and the way that you execute that plan. In military terms, and I haven't been in the military in a long time, so I'm just an observer, but the battlefield used to be red coats marching forward, kneeling, firing, very predictable, okay? And the way to win in that war was *pretty predictable. You know, have more bullets, have better discipline ...*

Ed: And overwhelming force ...

Bill: Bingo. Then the battlefield became really fluid, that's what General (Stanley) McCrystal came into ... this very fluid, digitally empowered battlefield. And it required an agile force.

So leadership can be delegated down to the lowest level. We communicated instantaneously to people ... all of a sudden, we went from getting our ass kicked by these digital Taliban warriors to beating the sh*t out of them ... that concept is what we bring to this so-called uncertain future.

Bill is pointing to what many people do not want to accept. They want the good ole predictable days, where change came slowly. It reminds me of the mindset idea that Carol Dweck wrote about back in the mid-2000s. She showed us how there were two mindsets, a growth one and a fixed one. Many people operate with a fixed mindset because it feels comfortable and secure. Other people operate with a growth mindset because they like being aggressive, always pushing forward to the next win.

I was asked about this during a presentation to a group of university leadership educators in Nairobi, Kenya earlier this year. In that moment, I realized that we had transitioned out of Carol Dweck's world into a new world. The days of choosing to have a fixed or growth mindset are over. Gone. Done. Growth doesn't come from overwhelming force. Staying the same doesn't preserve safety and security. We need a different mindset for a time of increasing uncertainty.

I asked Bill what he did to adapt to the uncertainty that the coronavirus pandemic brought to his business.

> On March 9th, we had an emergency internal meeting. I said, "We have four priorities now, I decided this over the weekend. I'm taking command."

Number one, we immediately have to become a "safe haven" for our employees. You will have a job. You will have full pay and we're going to work your butt off, so if your husband (we're a company of 100% women) loses his job or you lose your second job or your clients quit you (because we have a lot of 1099s), we won't.

While I was talking to them, I was wire transferring in a bunch of new capital, which is still sitting there. We never needed it. I asked our CEO, "What's in our bank account right now?" She logged on. She went, "Oh my gosh!" Then I said, "Exactly. I don't know how we're going to get through this, got no clue how bad it's going to be, maybe we lose all our Members in the next month, I don't know, but we're going to continue."

Number two, we're going to create a financial runway. I put in the new capital, so that now we've got emergency reserves.

Number three, we're going to become oxygen for our Members. We will be so helpful and valuable, they be able to imagine living without us. "I don't know what that looks like, but we're going to make it happen."

Then I said, "Once we get these three things done, we're going out to find more members to help, because that's what we do. We're built for this period of time, and so within two weeks, we had our situation room up online, we've have now maybe 30 or 40 free resources there. We've been running free workshops every Thursday for the public, and giving tons of helpful stuff away.

Number four, we immediately hired two people to work with members. We created products that they wanted, and we went forward.

I think the methodical structure, the methodical plan and the structured approach to resolving and accelerating issues, Ed, *and having proven resources that are just there for their using ... our members realized, when they didn't quit they were hoping that that's what they were going to get from us.*

Bill and his team's response wasn't either a fixed or growth mindset. It was instead an agile one. Uncertainty presents opportunities. It requires commitment and discipline. It demands change. The mindset is more than just what you want for your business. It goes well beyond it.

Here's the result of Bill's new four priorities.

We had at least one month of reduced revenue. This month (June) will be our highest month in history and next month should be even higher based on our current pipeline. It gives me confidence that I didn't always have because I perceived that potentially our services were discretionary ... that when things got bad, you know, people would jettison us quickly, like their country club dues or whatever. It's not what happened. We had a few alumni come back. Yes, we had some Members temporarily go on scholarship. They felt unstable economically, but they didn't want to lose us, so they asked, "Could we give them free tuition or something for a while?" We did. They got themselves through what they thought was going to be a difficult time. Now, a lot of them are thriving, which in turn, all but one has come back on full investment. So one of the risks of my business, I think is not as risky as I had perceived. The answer to your question is, we go forward with greater acceleration in Q3 and Q4 then we had anticipated... We still think we can make and exceed our annual plan, which we set last year.

Bill's story points to two important principles that are required in times of uncertainty. First is discipline and a method for functioning regardless of circumstances. That discipline requires focus and clarity about what is essential. Second is a commitment to people. Bill is not only committed to his Members, but to his teammates.

The Foundation of Self-Awareness

An agile mindset requires a foundation that is rock-solid, unshakable, and enduring through the transitions of uncertainty. It is something that I emphasize with Circle of Impact all the time. You must know who you are, what you believe, and why you are doing what you are doing. The values that comprise this foundation need to be non-negotiable. If your values and purpose are negotiable, then there is nothing you can depend upon. You are building your house, your life, our business on sand. You are going to be tossed around because your foundation is based on how you feel in the moment. Here's an example Bill shared with me.

> *A member asked me to attend their weekly tactical meeting yesterday. At 1:30 in the afternoon, alright. I was just going to be an observer. I was just going to comment on how they were doing. At 1:27, three minutes before their weekly tactical company meeting, 1:27pm, they called me and said, "Hey, Bill... Sh*ts really hitting the fan over here, you know, we're going to have to postpone our meeting, I hope you can join later, you know." Well, they never had it.*

I've seen this my entire career. People not only cancel meetings like this, but they cancel contracts. End relationships because they are in some panic mode that freaks them out. If you have ever been in this position, you need to change right now. Because the uncertainty that we have now is not going away. It is only going to get harder, tougher, and more confusing. I know, and Bill knows, that you don't want that. Focus on building a foundation of awareness that gives you the personal strength to say, "Start the meeting!"

We need a strong foundation so that we can respond confidently in the moment of uncertainty. The missing element for most of us is a lack of self-awareness. Over the past five years, I have spent a lot of time analyzing my experience in working with people. There always seemed to be something that made our projects less than successful. I finally came to realize that it was the self-perception of the CEO, the executive director, the owner, and, often, the entire staff.

If we allow ourselves to be defined by the work we do, or the skills we know, or the place where we work, then we are at the mercy of circumstances. There is no mercy. Just brutal reality.

In a static environment, we lower standards of performance in order to avoid having to change. No one ever fulfilled their potential by settling for the false security of a non-changing environment. In a culture of accelerating uncertainty, it is a recipe for crisis and chaos, fear, anxiety and loss. I'm not kidding. There is no safety in trying to avoid change. I've seen it and experienced in my family. There is no advancement in playing it safe.

The decisions that Bill made are based upon a strong foundation of values, purpose, and discipline. It has made him who he is and what The Lions Pride has become. Our conversation went deeper into this subject.

> *Bill: You brought up two points that resonated with me. One, the overarching way that our leaders are handling change in a dynamic organization. The only thing constant that is not changing is that the organization is constantly changing. Two, because the organization is growing, the organization is accelerating, and so that requires change.*

The Human Dimension

A key element in having the capacity to adapt to change as Bill demonstrates is being clear about the human dimension. Without clarity of awareness we can lose touch with why we are in business in the first place, and secondly, what it really takes to succeed, and thirdly, what leadership means in this 21st century context.

Bill: In the end, what is a business? It's just relationships with people in a capitalist society, an exchange of value. I provide you a product, you give me some money for it. It's human beings transacting with each other.

You know the saying that ... Well, it's not personal. It's just business. That's such the stupidest thing to say. It's not... It's always personal. We're always human beings dealing with other human beings. Even if I'm dealing with Amazon, there's a coder, there's a developer, there's a technologist on the other end creating my experience.

So I feel like I'm engaging with the website, but there really are people there. So every technological and digital problem that I may be facing in my life is created by a human being. Every solution that accelerates me... created by a human being. Whether it's in the conference room where I'm dealing with the problematic employee or whatever, or a piece of technology that's not working, it's a human problem. And so of course it could be broken coding and all that, but someone's got to fix it. And until AI gets to the point where it's self-fixes itself or robots run around, then we depend on people.

So the idea that it's only business, that doesn't go together. It's always human. So that's number one. And number two, for me to be the best human for you, I need to know what I am as a human. Self-awareness. That comes to what you just said, Ed, which is a self-awareness piece. It's the emotional deep dive. You know on the OPSP (One Page Strategic Plan*) and OP3

(One Page Personal Plan*), there's my core values, there are my life stories, there are my assessments, there is all sorts of stuff that helps me understand how I came here, how I am coming to you at the moment, and how I can be the best me so I can be the best for you. Not let my past, my negative past influence my present, it's not relevant. I can leave my negative past, it just made me who I am. So, it is about me getting awareness and especially if I'm a leader, and then engaging with you on a human level in a very authentic way. I think it is a gift.

For many people, they have never developed an understanding of who they are like Bill describes. It isn't just what I want or what skills I have. In understanding how I got here, I can learn where I want to go. A problem that I have encountered throughout my whole career is a resistance to knowing oneself with clarity and honesty because of some negative experience in the past. One of the products of the modern world is that more and more people have had traumatic experiences in their life. The trauma is not a personal flaw, but an experience. Uncertainty can be traumatic if you have built your life to avoid change. Trauma needs perspective, professional care, and a plan for turning it into an advantage. I have seen too much trauma to minimize the impact on people. I have also seen people triumph over it to create lives that flourish in the midst of the hardness of this world.

Self-understanding is not just what I can do, but why I react to uncertainty the way I do. If this sounds like a topic for discussion in a therapist's office, it is. It is also a reality that affects leaders and employees in the workplace. However, when you enter into a support process of developing your self-awareness, some distance to the trauma needs to be found. We see how it has come to define us. When we begin to see ourselves as we can be, not in what we must be, we discover a way to be agile and resilient in the midst of uncertainty. More from Bill on why it is important to create a strong foundation of understanding.

> *Bill: There were companies who, in March, rallied and bonded and those CEOS said,*

"We're in this together, and I don't know where we're going, but by God, I'm going down with the ship just like you are, I'm not first in a life boat." Then there were other companies that we read about that were cutting employees, putting people on unemployment while the CEO got paid a multi-million-dollar bonus.

Well, I get that we need CEOS and they're making tough decisions and blah, blah blah, so they earn their bonus ... But the optics on that are terrible. Terrible, just horrendous, and that CEO doesn't deserve to be in my mind a crisis leader. Cause they have bad judgment, that's all. I think number one, how do we handle change? Number two, how do we come to you as a human in a challenging situation, even if I'm the leader? And number three, who am I?

Gay Hendricks in his book, The Big Leap, writes about what he calls our upper limit problem. He describes four zones that we each can operate in. We each have a zone of incompetence, a zone of competence, a zone of excellence, and, a zone of genius. Imagine if your upper limit problem was due to you being totally ill-suited to perform the work of your job. I know many people who are in situation where they have never discovered their true selves because they are operating in either their zone of competence or excellence. They have never discovered what it is that they are better at than almost anyone else that they know.

What does it mean to live in your zone of genius? It means that you have identified what it is that is your unique contribution to the world. It is that thing that you and only you can give, and that you are the best at doing. For most people who are driven to excel, they do so at the expense of where their genius leads them. It is a key element in understanding how to live in an uncertain time.

Look at everything that you do during a given day or week. Ask: "Is there someone here that is better suited to do this task than me?" Or, you could ask, "What is it that I do that no one else can do that creates the impact that I can?" This is your zone of genius. It is an essential part of your self-awareness.

If we never discover this perspective our lives, we will spend our lives spinning our wheels trying to be someone we are not. If this can be true for you, for me, or for Bill, it can also be true for everyone you employ, for every member of your family, and your community. What, then, is your upper limit area of excellence that is the obstacle to your being the genius everyone you know needs you to be?

Just as individuals have their zone of genius, so do businesses. Is your business simply a copy or an imitation of a leader in your industry? Bill's business and mine are very different. They are because Bill's zone of genius is different from mine. Discover your zone of genius and you won't have to imitate someone else, finding yourself disappointed that you never achieved what they are able to do. You can lead the way through your own strength of genius.

This is just the starting point for creating a life and process of living that makes the midst of uncertainty a time of opportunity and impact. Next, we need a plan. Bill has that for us.

The Plan

Having spent two years in Bill's program, I discovered methods, tools, and, patterns of behavior that changed my life. I can tell you that it was hard, filled with challenges, critical mistakes, and, ultimately success. There is really no other way. Leadership is not just a mindset or a sense of awareness. It is a disciplined approach to "taking personal initiative to create impact that makes a difference that matters." If we only do that which makes us feel good, we'll never reach a place where we can feel good in the midst of the chaos of uncertainty.

> *Bill: First, you need to get centered in who you are as a leader, so that you are calm in your zone of genius to your teams and your employees and your customers, and your prospects, and your board and all that, comfortable in your own skin, not pretending... living super authentically. Not trying to be something that you're not ... just being more of what you are. Then, step two, you create a plan and, you lead your team through the plan. I told you about the 10X*

process that creates the OPSP ... Then, step three, you set up a high performance score board that tracks individual and company metrics. Lastly, you set up a meetings-that-don't-suck meeting rhythm to review the scoreboard, and you do that on a daily, weekly, quarterly basis. These three 10X steps are just the battle rhythm that you do day-in and day-out.

Who are you talking to and leading? If you do A Player Hiring, you are working with the A-Team. You and I have talked about that. You get A players on your team, and then very important, to get them, there's a structured process for that. ... Once you get the A player on, now you need to transition into clarity for that A player, and empowerment and engagement. The engagement comes from A Player Culture, that's the overarching umbrella of high-performance organizations. But the actual implementation tool is the truncated Job Scorecard with four things in it for each employee. Number one, it's key performance areas (KPAs)

- what they're very specifically responsible for. You're responsible for bringing us new leads. You're responsible for signing new customers. You're responsible for developing new products. Number two, how do we know that you're winning in that? KPI's - Key Performance Indicators. Key Performance are the daily, weekly, monthly, and annual measures that provide a reality mindset to the business. Number three, what resources do you need to win? And, lastly, what decisions do you need to keep winning all the time without being slowed down. Those four things.

So it's a truncated job scorecard, and then we create the organizational Accountability Chart, so that I know what Ed's doing. I'm clear about it. I know how Ed can help me. I know how I can help Ed. I know what Ed's working on this quarter. I know what Ed is working on this week.

Bill describes tools for managing people and processes. Bill's 10X Accelerator Playbook is a productivity and growth acceleration mindset and structured process. OPSP is the acronym for One Page Strategic Plan, a process developed by Vern Harnish that Bill has adapted to his program. My utilization of the OPSP has done more to advance my business than anything else. The adoption of the 10X mindset has helped me be more imaginative and realistic in my goals. The scoreboard and rhythm methodologies bring everyone together on the same page.

The A-player hiring process spearheaded by Dr. Brad Smart bases recruitment and employment on demonstrated past behavior. What is behavior? It is what can be observed and measured that reflects the values and character of a person.

Each one of these methodologies provide clarity, direction, and recognition about where we are in the midst of uncertainty. These are the skills and disciplines that lead to the agility that we need to be a leader for uncertain times.

Taking Personal Initiative to Create Change In the Midst of Chaos

An underlying belief that we share is the importance of taking personal responsibility. I have seen many organizational leaders bounce between passivity and passive aggression. These behaviors are toxic to their organizations. We could describe them operating along a spectrum between the two behaviors.

On the one end is the leader who refuses to take command or responsibility. I have the image in my mind of the leader who sits behind his desk, gives orders, and never follows up. When things fall apart, it is never his fault.

The other end of the spectrum is the leader who interferes with the company employees' work. Never knowing if any decision or action is correct, staff are paralyzed to act, always fearing a negative response. The purpose of the company revolves around the fractured ego of the leader. As a result, the leader is beyond accountability.

To take personal responsibility as a leader requires action. Action defines leadership. This is why I see that all leadership begins with personal initiative to create impact that makes difference that matters. Action translates mindset, self-awareness, intention into change. This is the change that I call impact. From this point-of-view, we can see how different approaches to leadership are applied. Bill describes.

Bill: Let's use the recent protests that are happening out on the streets to solve a huge … a macro level, multi-century, multi-decade at least, deeply embedded societal problem that requires a legal and political fix, a governmental fix. What we do know is this … governments move slow. Very slow. Legal System, very slow. And there's good reason for that.

What the protesters knew though was they could probably affect some immediate change with on-the-ground action.

We could have some meetings and create a political action committee to study this rac-

ism and inequality problem. Then we could try and elect the official and then get that elected official to put that change on their agenda once they're in office. We might be talking three, four, 10 years or whatever. What the protesters realized was, oh no, if we go protest, even violently … which I don't agree with … we can make change happen in Minneapolis with the city council, so that the next time they vote things start changing.

We are going to act. We're going to meet at 3 o'clock on Friday, and we're going to march over the weekend.

Bill is talking about taking action. Action defines who we are more than words do, more than marketing campaigns, or more than social media posts.

My life changed two decades ago when I realized that I needed to "stop talking about leadership, and lead." Within a matter of months, two significant opportunities to lead emerged. Taking action cemented all the scattered notions about leadership that I had been thinking for the previous two decades. Almost immediately, the frame work for my leadership model, Circle of Impact came to me. This is why my definition of leadership is that "all leadership begins with personal initiative to create impact that makes a difference that matters."

Let us be absolutely clear here. We take action to create change. The change we want is some impact that makes a difference that matters. We are not playing word games. This is about real change that impacts people, and groups, and communities.

In the following story, Bill describes a situation that affected one of his members. The question for us all is, if this person was our friend or colleague, what is the action that we individually should take?

This what I was telling our Cohort last month. I said, "Listen guys, gals, social injustice is a real deal. Apparently. I'm a white, very clueless, privileged male. How did I come to that realization? Okay, sorry to say, one of our Members told a story that I did not know that "A" (name delet-

ed), a West Point graduate, a Purple Heart, Bronze Star military vet was arrested in Atlanta because he was driving down the street. There was an APB out for a black man who looked like him. They didn't check his ID. They didn't. They just pulled him out of the car threw him on the hood, hand cuffed him, sat him on the ground and then questioned him. Then, after learning more about him, they released him. But the damage was done. And, that, right there, has never happen to me.

When I heard that story a month ago, I said, "Are you kidding me? Man, have I been clueless."

Awareness leads to commitment. Our commitment to action demands a plan. The plan is to be absolutely clear about the impact that we want to have. What is the change that you want? It cannot be about just exercising your own ego or emotions to feel like you are doing something that matters. It is being clear about what matters and focusing your intention and resources there. Your action plan marshals everyone who shares your vision of impact to join you in the action you are taking. This is what is happening on the streets with the protests. The question always remains. What is the impact that we want to create?

In addressing "A"'s situation, Bill focused the Cohort's attention.

> *Apparently, we have this problem. I've challenged the Cohort. Some are startups who have one employee, some of them have 30 employees. I said to them, "Okay, I don't know when the government is going pass a new whatever to address this, but we can sure change our companies, whatever that means, we can. I don't know what that means for your company, but that's what I want to explore in today's discussion. The point is ... do something ... now ... change your company, change your family, change your community, don't wait for the President or the Supreme Court. Let's change it."*

I was talking with friends this week about this. Their city had demonstrations that became violent destroying the store fronts of many downtown businesses. The community rallied and came to the aid of these small businesses. Crisis created compassion to care for people hurt by the protests. One type of action that was destructive produced a response of a second type of action which was restorative. We need a lot more of the second kind of response.

This is how you act in a time of uncertainty. You care for those closest to you first. You take care of your family, your employees, and local community. If you have any more capacity to care, you help people around the world.

This is why we need to be aware of what is going on in our communities. From there we can take action.

The Future is Local

When chaos descends upon a business, a family, or a community, you have to reorient by adjusting your perspective. I like to imagine focusing on that which is within an arm's reach. This is your local community. The structure of your business, the people you employ, your clients, even the vendors that serve your company, and foremost, your family and network of friends.

When the wagon trains crossed the continent to the West in the 19th century, they would circle the wagons at night as a means of protection. We are in a time where we need to circle the wagons of our local communities to support and protect the people who are most vulnerable.

For some of us, our local community is wherever we have close friends and colleagues. My local community is scattered around the world in places like Africa, India, Nepal and Pakistan, across Europe and the United States.

This focus on the local context of a business is a key to being agile. This is especially true if your business is under threat. It is a complicated time for many small, local businesses. The social orders that local and state governments have placed on businesses to reopen has meant for many that they will close.

What is the impact on a local community when a business closes? It may mean a family and employees must move away. Friendships are severed. Families split apart. It means a loss of tax revenue that communities need to pay for basic infrastructure needs. Communities are not a collection of business but an interdependent web of relationships that create the life of the community.

We need to support our local businesses so that they can find the agility they need to serve their customers and clients. Bill tells how a local baker here in Jackson responded to the coronavirus pandemic in a very agile, profitable way.

> *Bill: You know A, who owns ... restaurants. As soon as coronavirus hit, they were slowly limping along ... three locations were shut down starting in mid-March. In May, they had a record month. Why? Because they pivoted up their online business and their online marketing and their take out and their delivery. So in four weeks they began the recovery ... Yes, they laid a ton of people off ... Yes, they all got unemploy-*

ment and all that ... Yes. They're bringing them back. Did she employ some for take-out and all that, yes. Why did she have a record month? Because she drove revenue relentlessly into an agile pivot. They said, Well, sh*t, if we can't have the doors open, people are still eating, so let's go find them where they are. And that's what they did.

Ed: And when you have a tangible product like a croissant or a bagel... You can do that pretty easily.

Bill: You can.

Ed: But it's hard, it's still hard. I'm not suggesting that it's easy. Because when people can identify exactly what you have to offer, they already wanted it, they are just wanting to know how can I access that in a new way?

Bill: That is correct, Ed. Some, not some. Many companies have had to pivot, not only in their delivery. The restaurant group just pivoted their delivery model. Yes, and their ordering model. We still have restaurants here where they are closed. There's a bunch of them who are open, but you have to call them. No easy cashless online ordering. Then you have to walk in, and pay and pick up your food. Order and delivery model failure.

There are other companies who have had to pivot into new products, new services. Like , at my company, we developed four new products and, new services because we're a service business. In four weeks, four new services that are actually driving revenue now that we didn't have before. They were always in our three-year plan. But in March, we said, "We need to get these up and running NOW." I think many companies have had to do that. Some companies obviously are bigger and choose to be slower. It's more complex and stuff than we had.

Well, one thing is for certain ... When we admit that the one thing for certain about an uncertain future is our future is uncertain, then we ask the agile-focused question, "So what are we going do about it?"

Before "A" could change their order and delivery process, they had to change their own mind about what their business was about. It may seem that it is a subtle shift from in-store sales to virtual sales, but it isn't. It changes everything about how you approach the function of your business, your relationship with customers, and how you define success after the pivot. This is where you team gains a greater level of importance to creating the impact you want in the future.

The Future is We Together

Bill and I are both fans of General Stanley McChrystal. His world of military strategy and deployment during two of the longest wars in the United States history highlights how to face uncertainty. We all remember what the country was like after the 9/11 tragedy.

The world had suddenly taken a turn in a direction in which we were not prepared. It was more uncertain on September 12 than any of us had ever experienced. Imagine commanding your nation's armed forces in that moment.

It was in that moment that a new kind of leadership was needed. It was what I had been seeing emerging since the mid-1980s. It wasn't about "the heroic CEO" but about how we all join together a team of leaders to move forward.

> *Bill: General McChrystal reinvented our Intelligence Network, which included FBI, White House, CIA, Delta Force, Rangers ...*
>
> *It was a multi-year process and he made tons of changes very fast and super effectively, but in the end, he realized... So let's say he's two or three years in, I don't exactly know, but he realized that the next step was him, that he was a block to the speed and velocity and effectiveness that was needed.*

Here's what he said. "Okay, we've given you all the information. We have shared information. We have shared consciousness. You know what Delta is working on, and you know who Delta is, and you know the Marines aren't the bad guy, and the White House isn't stupid. Now we have shared respect, shared consciousness, shared communication, shared information in real time. What we don't have yet in a lot of cases is shared empowerment. If you want to do X, Y, Z, you have to get higher up approval, and that takes time. In some cases, I'm the approval guy. I hold these decisions for my approval. That ends as of today. Here's what you got to do? Ask the questions: Does this fulfill the mission? Is it ethical? Is it moral? Is it legal? Check those boxes. If you can't get a hold of somebody else, take action. That was the final thing that he did, that he professes and is validated by other leaders who were with him, that increased not only the velocity, the speed, but the effectiveness of the fighting force.

What you just said is exactly that. In other words, we failed if we've not unleashed our A Players to deliver their best, consistent with, does it fulfill the mission, is it legal, ethical, and moral? Go, let me see what you can do.

I think Ed, then what we do we see? A Players so excited, so energized and so impactful, that we then fulfill our mission.

How do you move from a leadership-starved business context where everything is on you, and no one is taking personal initiative to create impact that makes a difference that matters? How do you create a leader-rich culture where everyone is seeing the big picture, seeing the future, seeing the whole challenge before you?

You have to respect and trust your people that they will give their best not in response to orders, but in response to the freedom to give their best. The kind of leadership General McChrystal instituted is what I call "CEO as Leadership Facilitator."

I learned this in a much less critical organizational situation. Two decades, without any preparation I was thrust into the role of scoutmaster for my son's scout troop. On that first night, I told my sons, "I don't know what I am doing here. I need you to tell me what we need. We are going to debrief every week as we drive home." It was a very uncertain moment. Two years later, the troop had grown from 15 scouts to 48. My adult leadership team had grown from three to 19. It was the kind of chaos every leader wants. I was a raw rookie recruit as scoutmaster. Here's what I did.

I established an understanding of who we were as a scout troop. Five principles that can easily be translated to any team.

1. Every scout will learn leadership.

2. Every scout will advance in rank.

3. Every scout will have fun.

4. We will teach leadership through the camping program.

5. We will all wear the scout uniform as a symbol of unity and strength.

I talked about these principles every week, and every chance I could get. Because I only wanted scouts and adults involved who believed in these principles. After a year, we expanded these principles to include every adult. The key insight is that as an organizational leader you are the chief story teller of the values that unite you as a team.

The second thing I did was I released each adult leader to do take responsibility in the area were they had an interest. They became the defacto leader of that program. They reported to me. I did not direct them. They directed me. They knew their job better than I did. I trusted them to do it.

I realized like General McChrystal that I in my role as scoutmaster was the principal obstacle to success of the troop. We would only succeed by my getting out of the way and letting our adult leaders fulfill their potential as adult scouters. As a result, the 19 men and women became a powerhouse of mentorship to the scouts. My role was to coordinate, facilitate, and remind all of us of the principles that defined us a troop. As a result, the troop became one of the strongest in our council.

What Bill and I are seeking to communicate here is that the nature of leadership has changed. It is not just being a strategist, a decision-maker, a delegator of work, and the boss over everyone. Smart leaders now understand that if they do not create an environment that elevates the leadership capacities of their people that they will never win the game. This shift to being a facilitator of your employees' leadership impact is illustrated in how Bill has structured his business, The Lion's Pride.

Ed: I was in Nairobi in February, speaking to 100 HR people at Standard Chartered Bank. Big bank that serves 88 countries. I'm standing there towards the end of the presentation, I said, "So we need to re-structure our companies by developing the leadership capacities of everyone... the HR director who was just sitting right to my right, almost jumped out of his seat. ... that's exactly what we need to do. He just loved it. ... So the question is, what does he do to facilitate the restructuring of his department to enable the development of the leadership capacities of all these people?

That's the question that I posed to him, but it's the same question that I would pose to a guy that runs a bakery in Denver, or a person who has a nail salon in Las Vegas. How do you take these things that we're talking about and actually equip them for your people, because we are at a transition point ... there are a lot of people who are entrenched in their positions of privilege of wealth and power who have outlived their value to their company. The only way to solve this problem is not to replace them, because the system, the structure, is not prepared to receive new ideas. You have to build from the bottom up, it's all bottom up, and it's all local. And that's what I see as our future.

And, Bill, that's your sweet spot, and that's why I believe in you, that's why I'm a huge fan of your work.

Bill: Well Ed, one of your basic tenants of your framework is that all change is local.

Ed: Yes.

Bill: Similar to my little treatise on not waiting for whatever it is at the macro level to sweep up from headquarters in order to initiate change. The protesters said, "Nope, I'm not waiting. I'm showing up at the corner of x and y and I'm marching and I'm doing something, but I'm not sitting on my ass." There were articles in The New York Times about adult children who went out to protest who happened to be living with their parents because of the coronavirus or whatever. They were going out. The parents said, "Why are you doing this? You should just let the system work." There were these articles, these journalistic exposes on these people from this generation that wanted to let the system fix it. Then the others who are like your tribe, Ed, who said "No, change is happening locally, and I'm part of it. I can't sit here and watch it on the news, I need to go do something."

And so, I agree with you 1 million percent, Ed, which is not possible, so 100%, that whether you're a nail salon or a bakery or whatever, you institute and accelerate, change.

Road to change? I'll give you one example.

There's a book called The Dream Manager, and it talks about this idea of business leaders who embrace and enable the dreams of their employees. When they do that, then the dreams of the company and the dreams of the leaders and all that become reality too. I embrace that, and I believe that when we show employees that they're not just people, just task doers that we want to show up and do, punch things and paint nails and that's it. See ya later, thanks for coming.

But when we know that they are human beings, we connect with them on the human level. They have dreams and hopes. That's when we really engage people. That is when we have high engagement. The research shows we have incredibly, noticeably, more powerful performance than the companies that don't have engagement.

So here's the deal. Quick example, Ina has been working with me since 2013. She's our designer. She's everything creative. Not writing, not words, but design.

She's awesome. She's got a great story. She's been accelerating her career with us and we've been benefiting in incredible ways. We read the Dream Manager and implemented its concepts. We called it your top 100 dreams. Kind of like your bucket list. Dream number 17 on her list was this really bad-ass motorcycle. And because of our Dream Fund, meaning our profit sharing program, we call it The Dream Fund, she received delivery. What's today, Thursday? Tuesday. She informed us that *for a year she had been making payments, and she made the final payment on Friday of last week, and we got a video Tuesday morning of her kicking it on. She fired up the engine. You think she's excited? She said to the team in the video, "Thank you for helping one of my dreams come true."*

Ed: I love that.

Bill: This is local change Ed, this helps enable people ... Who identifies, recognizes, and encourages... who enables that dream to come true. Even if it's not financial, even if it's just encouragement and Hey, how you doing on your GED? And whatever it the dream is for the employee.

The Certainty of Uncertainty

Everything Bill and I have discussed in this short book relates to businesses, families and communities in any kind of situation. We could have had the same conversation and never mentioned change, transition or uncertainty. This is because the programs we each provide to our clients are foundational to success. They aren't band-aids for people feeling uncertain. This is business equivalent of strengthening your body's immune system so it fights the virus of uncertainty, fear, and doubt.

The issues of uncertainty are real, and are increasing. Do not believe that the current trajectory of society will continue like this. In many respects, it doesn't matter. Because when you decide to be the leader of a team of leaders, of a community of persons of impact, then whether things are certain or not doesn't matter. You are not driving change. You are driving impact that makes a difference that matters.

It is not a choice between a growth or fixed mindset. It is a choice to elevate every situation to fulfill its potential regardless of the challenges in front of you. Three times in the past twenty five years, I lost all my clients in a matter of weeks. The third time, following the Great Recession of 2008, eventually brought me to the point where I had to close my consulting practice. Then my marriage ended, followed shortly by my termination as executive director of a non-profit organization. Not just losing clients, but losing the institutions that I had invested my life in. Was the time uncertain? Certainly. What did I do? I made a decision. I knew that if I was to make something of the rest of my life, I had to move and start over. I did and I never looked back.

Even now as a coach and writer, I am constantly pivoting to reframe how I going to meet the needs of the marketplace. Having watched Bill train and coach his clients over the years, he is helping them do the same. You have seen it in his thoughts shared here.

We want this short book to inspire you to take action. But inspiration in the midst of uncertainty is kind of like a hyper-sugary soda on a hot day. It tastes great for the moment then the sugar high drops your energy like a rock. You go looking for more inspiration. There is never enough inspiration to create the impact that your potential predicts. I'll give Bill the last word.

I think all motivational books fail in actual implementation.

When you go and walk on fire with Tony Robbins, you are inspired and motivated until you go home Sunday night and things are still the same. You wake up Monday morning, and your world is still a black hole of gravity that holds you right where you are. It's why most lottery winners are poor in a year or two. It is why most people who lose weight then gain weight, gaining more weight back than they had. ... There are so many examples of that, Ed. I think being the author that you are, you combine this beautiful ability to inspire people to change at the localist level. But then you empower and enable them to actually drive change. Because a lot of people are motivated, but then what? Then what? Motivation must convert into action and action converts to change.

Ed: That is the question, what is the impact they want?

Bill: Most people who want change say to themselves (or should), I'm not hanging around with the people that are going to empower me to change. I don't have any tools or resources or background to do it. Google just delivered 1.7 million answers to, 'how do I make change happen?' Ed, you're going give them a simple formula in your books.

Then you're going to say, "You want more?" Contact me. Then you're going drive even more change to those percentage of people who are truly serious. I do the same ... This is how it happens, whether you're doing it in the UK or the US or Africa or whatever, it's getting them locked and loaded emotionally. Empower them to say, "Yes, I want to retire, I want to have a farm, I want to have income ... And this action is how I'm going do it." Take the first step. Forward

Call To Action

Bill and I are both coaches. We approach the process very differently. We are here to help you find a path that thrives in the midst of uncertainty.

It all begins with answering a simple question.

What do you want to change?

Answering this questions leads to self-awareness, a purpose for impact, and a set of methodologies that can carrying your through.

We are here to help. All you have to do is ask.

This is one thing about which we are both absolutely certain.

Who is Bill Watkins?

In 1994, Bill built a garage-based startup that he transformed into an 8-figure valuation—and sold it for cash in 2012. And two years later, he turned his tools and experience into a 10x Acceleration phenomenon that helps high-performing Founder CEOs achieve faster, better, and easier success—with fewer speed bumps.

Find Bill at The Lions Pride - http://thelionspride.com/

Who is Ed Brenegar?

Ed is a global thought leader, coach, trainer and speaker. His purpose is to inspire and equip people world-wide to take personal initiative to create impact in their local communities. He provides training and coaching for people to assist their organizations and their communities to become leader-rich places of impact. He is the author of Circle of Impact: Taking Personal Initiative To Ignite Change. He lives in Jackson Hole, Wyoming.

Find Ed at Circle of Impact Leadership - https://edbrenegar.com

What are The Transition Chronicles?

We all live in a time of transition. It is different than just recognizing that change is happening. It is seeing that transition is a process along a path of change. The more we embrace the transitions that we are in, the more we can thrive in a time of uncertainty. The Transition Chronicles is an ongoing series of short books (5,000 to 12,000 words in length) that focus on various aspects of the transitions that we experience through the three dimensions of the Circle of Impact. All the Chronicles will first be made available as Amazon Kindle downloads. Later, softcover versions will be made available.

For more information about the series, even suggesting a topic for me to consider, you can contact me at ed@edbrenegar.com. Please either put the title of the short book or the series in the subject heading.